A Marshall Edition
Edited and designed by Marshall Editions
The Orangery
161 New Bond Street
London W1Y 9PA

Original concept by Mike Foster

This edition first published by Scholastic Inc.
555 Broadway, New York, NY 10012
SCHOLASTIC and associated logos are trademarks and/or
registered trademarks of Scholastic Inc.

10 9 8 7 6 5 4 3 2 1   8 9/9 0/0 01 02 03

Library of Congress Cataloging-in-Publishing data available.

ISBN 0-590-11919-2

Consultant, United States:
Dr. Carol A. Benson
Andrew W. Mellon Fellow, Ancient Art
The Walters Art Gallery
Baltimore, Maryland.

Consultant, United Kingdom:
Felicity Cobbing
Palestine Exploration Fund, London.
Formerly of the British Museum,
Department of Western Asiatic Antiquities.

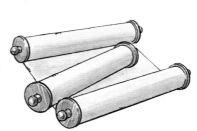

Artwork assistant: Carl Venton, Maltings Partnership.

Printed and bound in Portugal
by Printer Portugesa.
Originated in the UK
by Jade Reprographics.

First Scholastic printing,
January 1999

The Traveler's Guide to
ANCIENT ROME

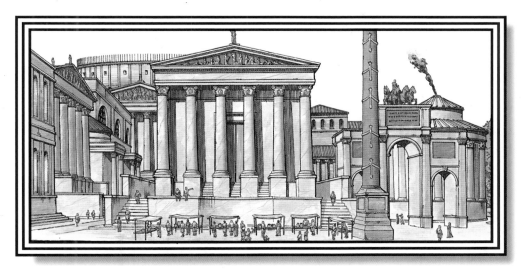

Written by JOHN MALAM
Illustrated by MIKE FOSTER

Scholastic Inc.
New York • Toronto • London • Auckland • Sydney

UNDERSTANDING DATES

Many historians use a calendar that divides the past into two separate eras: B.C. (before Jesus Christ) and A.D. (Latin initials that mean "The Year of our Lord"). They call the year that Jesus Christ was born "1 A.D." They count forward from year 1 in the A.D. era, and backward from year 1 in the B.C. era. The Romans counted their years from 753 B.C. onward—the year they thought Rome was founded. So, to a Roman, the year A.D. 320 would be the year 1073 A.U.C. This stands for Ad Urbe Condita, meaning "from the founding of the city."

THE DATE OF YOUR VISIT

This guidebook looks at Rome during the time of Emperor Constantine (reigned A.D. 307 to 337), which was when the city reached its greatest size, with perhaps one million residents.

KEY TO ABBREVIATIONS

km = kilometer/kilometre
m = meter/metre
ft = foot/feet
cm = centimeter/centimetre
g = gram/gramme
lb = pound
oz = ounce
kg = kilogram/kilogramme
l = liter/litre

CONTENTS

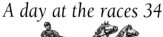

H ail, stranger! Or as the Romans say, *"Salve, hospes!"* Listen for these words of friendship as you walk along the city's busy streets— the Romans pride themselves on giving only the best hospitality, and you will be made most welcome in this great city.

Rome has something for everyone—taverns, baths, shops and markets, theaters, and racetracks. If you decide to settle here, one day you will be able to say: *"Civis Romanus sum"*—"I am a Roman citizen."

Emperor Constantine

From its humble origins as a hill village of thatched huts near the Tiber River, Rome has grown into the grandest city in the world.

For 200 years Rome was ruled by kings. There followed 500 years of the Roman Republic, when Rome was governed by the people. During this time Rome became Italy's leading city. In 27 B.C., Augustus became Rome's first emperor, and the Roman Empire began. From then on, Rome gained control of many faraway lands, and the city prospered.

Today, in the reign of Emperor Constantine, Rome is still a great city. He has enriched the city with fine new buildings, which you will be able to see on your visit to this grand capital. Enjoy your stay!

TIMELINE

1,000–264 B.C.

c. 1,000 B.C.
The first settlers arrive on the Palatine hill, one of the seven hills on which the city of Rome is later built.

753–509 B.C.
According to legend, Rome is founded in 753 B.C. Romulus is Rome's first king. Six more kings ruled after Romulus.

264–27 B.C.

27 B.C.
The Roman Republic ends and the Roman Empire begins. Augustus becomes the first emperor, head of state for Rome.

47–44 B.C.
In 47 B.C. Julius Caesar declares himself dictator, or sole ruler, for 10 years, but is murdered after three years.

27 B.C.–A.D.117

c. 6 B.C.
Jesus Christ is born in the Roman province of Judea.

A.D. 64
A great fire that burns for nine days destroys much of Rome. Emperor Nero blames the Christians.

A.D. 117–324

A.D. 324
The city of Constantinople is founded by Emperor Constantine.

A.D.324–1453

A.D. 395
The empire is divided into two parts: the west, ruled from Rome; and the east, ruled from Constantinople.

A.D. 410
Barbarian Visigoths sack the city of Rome and the empire starts to collapse.

509 B.C.
Rule by kings ends and the Roman Republic begins. Two consuls are approved by the people and serve for one year only.

390 B.C.
Barbarian Gauls from the north attack Rome.

378 B.C.
Walls are built around Rome.

334–264 B.C.
Rome fights her neighbors in Italy and wins control of all the country south of the Po River.

73–71 B.C.
A slaves' revolt in southern Italy, led by Spartacus, threatens Rome, but is defeated.

218–202 B.C.
An army from Carthage, a city in north Africa, invades Italy. The Romans defeat Hannibal, the Carthaginian leader, at the Battle of Zama.

312 B.C.
The *Aqua Appia*, Rome's first aqueduct, and the *Via Appia*, the first significant road, are built.

A.D. 79
In the south of Italy, Mt. Vesuvius erupts and destroys Pompeii and other towns.

A.D. 80
The Colosseum in Rome is opened.

A.D. 112–13
Trajan's Forum and Trajan's Column are opened in Rome.

A.D. 117
Emperor Trajan dies. Under his rule, the Roman Empire was at its largest.

A.D. 313
Emperor Constantine allows Christians to practice their religion openly.

A.D. 310–13
The Basilica of Constantine is built in Rome.

A.D. 165–67
Plague spreads through the empire.

A.D. 212–16
The Baths of Caracalla are built in Rome.

A.D. 455
Barbarian Vandals sack Rome.

A.D. 476
Romulus Augustulus is the last emperor of the western part of the empire. The empire in the west ends. Barbarians from northern Europe take control of Rome.

A.D. 1453
Constantinople is captured by the Turks. The empire in the east ends.

Note
The *c.* in a date, such as c. 1,000 B.C., is an abbreviation for *circa*, the Latin word for "about" or "around."

YOUR VISIT

Traveler—your visit to Rome comes at a turning point in the history of the Roman Empire. Emperor Constantine, who spends much time in Constantinople, the empire's new capital, has tried to keep the empire together. But his fear is that it will soon be invaded by tribes of ruthless barbarians. There is danger inside the empire too, with Roman generals trying to gain control of some of the lands. Despite this, Rome is still the empire's beating heart—a tourist attraction without rival!

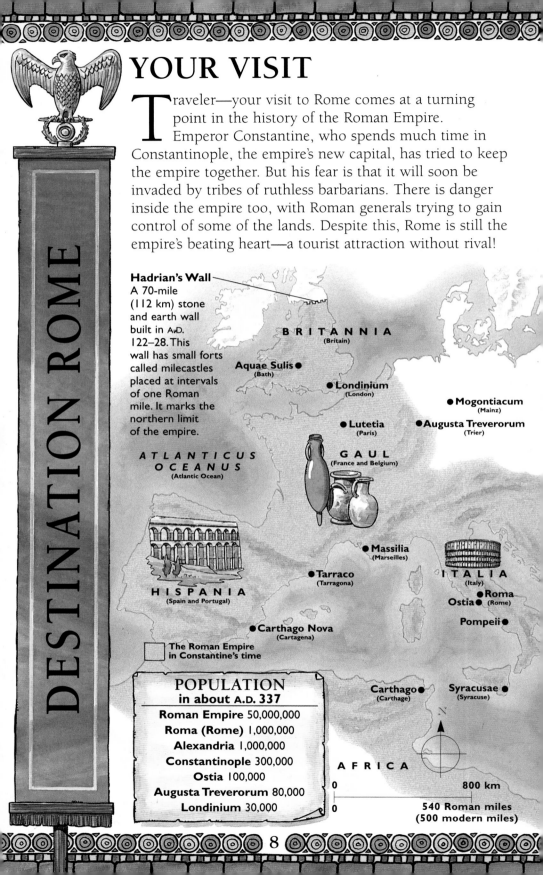

Hadrian's Wall
A 70-mile (112 km) stone and earth wall built in A.D. 122–28. This wall has small forts called milecastles placed at intervals of one Roman mile. It marks the northern limit of the empire.

B R I T A N N I A
(Britain)

Aquae Sulis ●
(Bath)

● **Londinium**
(London)

● **Mogontiacum**
(Mainz)

● **Lutetia**
(Paris)

● **Augusta Treverorum**
(Trier)

A T L A N T I C U S
O C E A N U S
(Atlantic Ocean)

G A U L
(France and Belgium)

● **Massilia**
(Marseilles)

I T A L I A
(Italy)

● **Roma**
(Rome)

Ostia ●

● **Tarraco**
(Tarragona)

H I S P A N I A
(Spain and Portugal)

Pompeii ●

● **Carthago Nova**
(Cartagena)

☐ The Roman Empire
in Constantine's time

Carthago ●
(Carthage)

Syracusae ●
(Syracuse)

N

POPULATION
in about A.D. 337
Roman Empire 50,000,000
Roma (Rome) 1,000,000
Alexandria 1,000,000
Constantinople 300,000
Ostia 100,000
Augusta Treverorum 80,000
Londinium 30,000

A F R I C A

0   800 km

0   540 Roman miles
(500 modern miles)

▼ *If you jumped forward to the present day (map below), you would find that Rome is the capital city of Italy. The city's population of three million people speaks Italian. Within Rome is the Vatican City, the heart of the Roman Catholic Church.*

CLIMATE AND LANDSCAPE

Temperature (Rome)
January: average 52°F (11°C)
July: average 85°F (29°C)
September: average 78°F (25.5°C)

Days of sunshine (Rome)
January: 7 days
July: 26 days
September: 24 days

Rainfall (Rome)
January: 2½ inches (6.3 cm)
July: ½ inch (1.2 cm)
September: 2 inches (5 cm)

Seasons (Rome)
Spring: warm and showery
Summer: very hot and dry
Fall: warm, with rain
Winter: cold

Highest Mountain (Italy)
Mont Blanc 15,771 ft (4,807 m)

Highest Waterfall (Italy)
Frua Cascade 470 ft (143.25 m)

Longest Rivers (Italy)
Po River 405 miles (652 km)
Tiber River 252 miles (406 km)

Greece
Before the Romans, the last major civilization in the Mediterranean area belonged to the Greeks, who reached their height of power around 400 B.C. The Romans have been their rulers since 146 B.C. and have learned much from them.

Constantinople
In A.D. 330 Emperor Constantine made the old Greek city of Byzantium the new capital of the Roman world. It is now called New Rome, or Constantinople.

PONTUS EUXINUS
(Black Sea)

●**Naissus**
(Nis)

●**Constantinople**
(Istanbul)
●**Nicomedia**
(Izmit)

MACEDONIA
(Macedonia)

ACHAEA
(Greece)

ASIA MINOR

Antiochia●
(Antioch)

●**Athenae**
(Athens)

MARE INTERNUM
(Mediterranean Sea)

J U D E A

THE SEVEN HILLS OF ROME

The city of Rome began life as a small hut village in the part of Italy known as Latium. There, alongside the Tiber River, was a group of seven low hills. The first people in the area lived in villages on the Palatine and Quirinal hills. In the 750s B.C., the villages joined together—and this was the start of Rome.

Alexandria●

CYRENAICA
(Libya)

A E G Y P T U S
(Egypt)

KEY TO MAP

- ■ RELIGIOUS SITES
- ■ FOOD
- ■ SPORTS
- ■ BATHS
- □ THEATERS
- ▭ ROADS

HOW TO GET AROUND

By litter

Six or eight tall porters, called *calones,* will carry you in style and comfort around the city.

By horse

You can hire a horse for traveling outside Rome. Main roads have relay stations where the horse can be changed.

By carriage

Travel in luxury along the *Via Appia* in a fully carpeted carriage drawn by the finest horses.

TOUR OF ROME

Roma
Rome's own goddess and guiding spirit. She holds a globe of the world in her hand.

The city of Rome is a beautiful and exciting place to visit. It has taken more than 1,000 years of building and rebuilding to create today's modern city of shining white marble. Standing proud above the city is the Imperial Palace, built on the Palatine hill where long ago Romulus decided to begin his city. Emperor Constantine's survey shows that there are now 28 libraries, 8 bridges, 11 public baths, 2 circuses, 2 amphitheaters, 290 warehouses, 1,352 fountains, 144 public lavatories, and 46,602 private houses!

▼ *The Pantheon is Rome's temple to all the gods. It is a marvel of the Roman Empire, built of concrete and stone. As you gaze in awe at its dome rising to the sky, without any visible means of support, you will wonder if the gods themselves hold it up.*

THE PANTHEON pp 16–17

▶ *You will find the Theater of Marcellus on the banks of the Tiber, near the bridge that crosses the river to Tiber Island. Why not be the first in your family to see a new play? It might be years before the show comes to your own local theater.*

THEATER OF MARCELLUS pp 30–31

Aurelian Wall

Pantheon

Baths of Nero

Stadium of Domitian

Theater of Pompey

Theater of Marcellus

Fabrician Bridge

The Tiber
Rome's fast-flowing river is crossed by many bridges. If you fall ill, then take the Fabrician Bridge to Tiber Island, where you will find a temple to the god of healing.

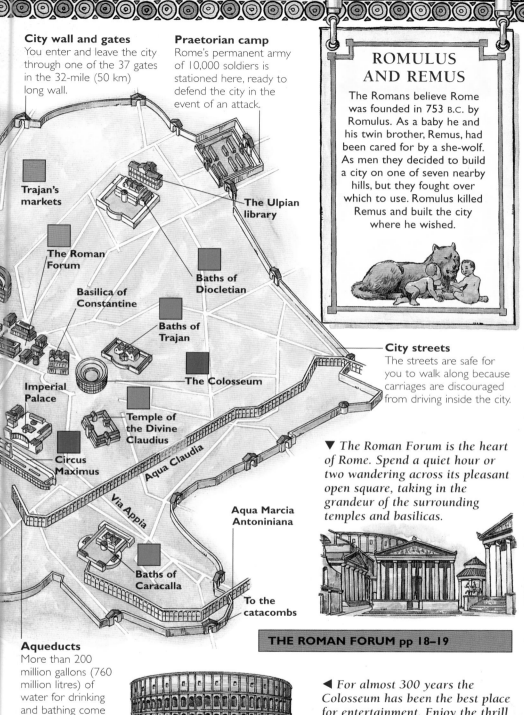

City wall and gates
You enter and leave the city through one of the 37 gates in the 32-mile (50 km) long wall.

Praetorian camp
Rome's permanent army of 10,000 soldiers is stationed here, ready to defend the city in the event of an attack.

ROMULUS AND REMUS

The Romans believe Rome was founded in 753 B.C. by Romulus. As a baby he and his twin brother, Remus, had been cared for by a she-wolf. As men they decided to build a city on one of seven nearby hills, but they fought over which to use. Romulus killed Remus and built the city where he wished.

Trajan's markets

The Ulpian library

The Roman Forum

Baths of Diocletian

Basilica of Constantine

Baths of Trajan

Imperial Palace

The Colosseum

City streets
The streets are safe for you to walk along because carriages are discouraged from driving inside the city.

Temple of the Divine Claudius

Circus Maximus

Aqua Claudia

Via Appia

Aqua Marcia Antoniniana

▼ The Roman Forum is the heart of Rome. Spend a quiet hour or two wandering across its pleasant open square, taking in the grandeur of the surrounding temples and basilicas.

Baths of Caracalla

To the catacombs

THE ROMAN FORUM pp 18–19

Aqueducts
More than 200 million gallons (760 million litres) of water for drinking and bathing come into the city every day by way of 19 aqueducts.

◄ For almost 300 years the Colosseum has been the best place for entertainment. Enjoy the thrill of the hunt, as beastfighters chase lions, tigers, and bears around the sandy arena. Or gasp in disbelief as Rome's gladiators fight to the death with nets, spears, and swords.

COLOSSEUM pp 32–33

FOOD AND LODGINGS

Visitors to Rome will find a good choice of places in which to stay, from comfortable town houses to noisy taverns and cramped rooms in apartment buildings. There is something for everyone, but shop around to make sure you are not being overcharged. The best rooms to look for are those close to water supplies, where the water you receive is more likely to be fresh; the worst ones are furthest away. And when it's time to eat, you might be invited to a banquet where, according to the custom, there will be nine guests and lots of excellent food and wine. At other times pop in to a *popina* for a quick snack—these eating houses can be found all over the city.

Fish sauce
Food is flavored with sauces, especially one made by boiling salt water, fish, and herbs in an earthenware cooking pot. The end result is a salty fish sauce called *garum*.

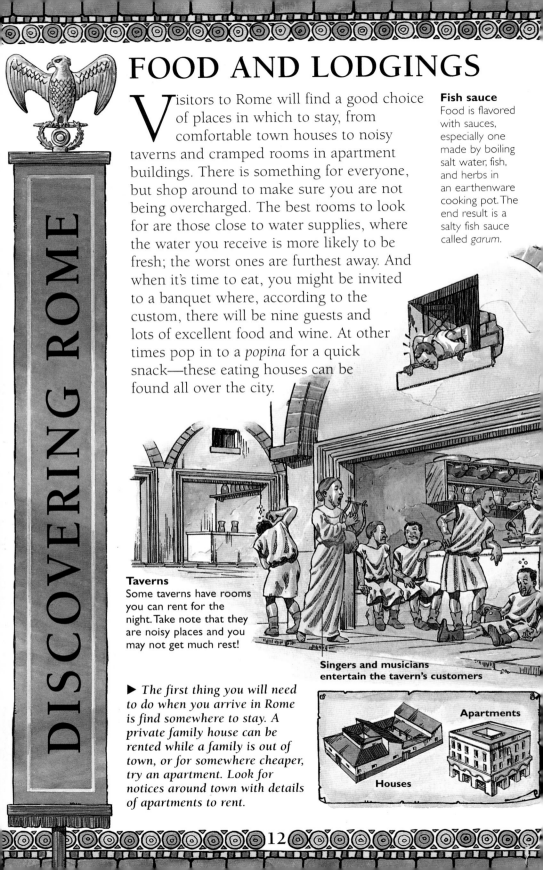

Taverns
Some taverns have rooms you can rent for the night. Take note that they are noisy places and you may not get much rest!

Singers and musicians entertain the tavern's customers

▶ *The first thing you will need to do when you arrive in Rome is find somewhere to stay. A private family house can be rented while a family is out of town, or for somewhere cheaper, try an apartment. Look for notices around town with details of apartments to rent.*

Apartments

Houses

▶ This menu is what you can expect to enjoy if you are lucky enough to be invited to a banquet in the house of a wealthy citizen. You will start eating at four o'clock in the afternoon, and the meal will last for three hours.

THREE-COURSE BANQUET

FIRST COURSE
(*gustatio*—starter)
Freshly caught shellfish and oysters drizzled in garlic sauce, snails cooked in their shells, sliced boiled eggs, lettuce, olives, figs, and honeyed wine.

SECOND COURSE
(*caput cenae*—main dish)
Whole roast boar, filled with sausages and egg yolks, followed by stuffed dormice in honey, peacocks, fish and shellfish, sauces, cabbage, and scented wine.

THIRD COURSE
(*secunda mensa*—dessert)
Fresh figs, pears, apples, grapes, olives, nuts, jam, pastries, and sweet wine.

The kitchen
Kitchen pots and pans have to be strong enough to withstand a lot of use. Unlike the fine pottery and glass vessels used at the table, items used to prepare food are made from coarse pottery, metal, and wood.

Large pots called *amphorae* store wine and oil

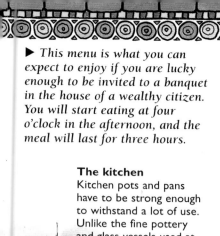

▲ Most Romans eat in the city's taverns. You will find them on the open-sided ground floors of apartment buildings. There is a good choice of food served all day long—peas and cabbage, barley gruel, and boiled sheep's heads in garlic and onion sauce are some of the specialities. Bread is eaten with most meals.

A ROMAN DINNER PARTY

If you are invited to a dinner party at the home of a Roman citizen, be sure to follow these standard rules of etiquette. You do not want to offend your host!

Remove outdoor shoes and put on sandals. A slave will wash your hands and place a crown of flowers on your head. At the table, lie on a couch, resting on your left elbow. Eat with your fingers.

●

It is good manners to throw up between courses, to make room for more food. Bring a feather to tickle your throat.

●

Stay for games and songs, before collecting your shoes and leaving.

Out

In

Men
Emperor Constantine has set a new fashion for men's hairstyles. Out have gone the old-fashioned beards made popular by emperors such as Hadrian. Today's men prefer the clean-shaven look with hair combed straight, not curled.

Out

In

Women
Waves and braids are popular at the moment. Elaborate hairdos with high crests of curls are no longer worn by the fashion-conscious. They now prefer their hair combed back in simpler styles. Blonde hair is still in fashion. Roman women use vinegar and olive oil to dye their brown hair.

WHAT TO WEAR

The Romans have a highly organized class system. You will meet people from all levels of society—you can tell them apart by their clothing styles. Citizens from wealthy families wear the latest fashions, just to let everyone know their position in society. Those from poorer families, and slaves, wear simpler, cheaper clothes made from poor quality fabric. Note that styles soon go out of fashion, as has happened with the *toga* and *stola*, so check your wardrobe before you come!

Children's clothes
Children wear similar clothes to adults. However, during a coming-of-age ceremony, 16-year-old boys wear a purple-edged toga of youth, which they swap for a plain white toga, symbolizing adulthood.

Charmed life
From birth until the age of 16, a boy wears a gold or leather charm called a *bulla* around his neck to ward off evil.

Gold *bulla*

▼ *Expensive items of jewelry are made from gold, silver, and polished stones such as garnets (red) and sapphires (blue). Cheaper jewelry is made from bronze and glass. Both men and women wear rings. Brooches fasten clothes together.*

Cameos

Brooches

Bracelets

Rings

Chains and necklaces

Stripy dress
Women wear the *dalmatica*. This long-sleeved, ankle-length tunic can be made from silk, linen, or wool. It is usually decorated with broad purple stripes called *clavi*.

THE TOGA
The *toga* is now only worn in court, yet in the early years of the empire it was the standard item of everyday dress for men. Made from a large piece of semicircular woolen cloth, the wearer needs help to drape a *toga* around him. An ordinary person's *toga* is white; an official's has a purple edge, and a black *toga* is worn at a time of mourning.

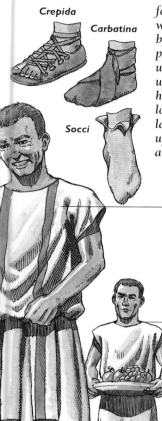

Crepida

Carbatina

Socci

◄ *There are leather shoes for indoor and outdoor wear. The* carbatina, *worn by peasants, is a single piece of ox-hide placed under the foot and tied up by thongs. The* crepida *has a tough sole, and side loops through which a lace is passed to tie it up. Loose-fitting* socci *are worn indoors.*

Belt up
Men wear the *colobium*. This is a knee-length linen tunic with short sleeves. It is considered untidy for a man to wear his *colobium* in public without a belt.

The family slaves
Roman families have different slaves for different tasks. Some have special duties at banquets, while others are employed to run the family home.

◄ *The family is the most important unit in Roman society. To the Romans, the word* familia *means a father, mother, and their children, together with their slaves and close relatives.*

Drape a *toga* over the left shoulder

An official's *toga*

WOMEN'S CLOTHING AND BEAUTY

Clothes of yesteryear

Palla

Stola

Stola

Palla over a stola

It was once the fashion for Roman women to wear the *stola* and the *palla*—but now, like the men's *toga*, both are old-fashioned. The *stola* was a long gown with a belt. The *palla* was a woolen wrap, worn over a *stola*, and draped around the body. It could be drawn up to cover the head, like a scarf.

Beauty preparations

Fashionable Roman women (and some men too) wear makeup. A fair complexion is thought especially beautiful—use chalk powder or white lead to whiten the skin, then add red rouge to the cheeks and lips. Line the eyes and eyebrows with black ash. Cover up blemishes with stick-on cloth patches, called *splenia*.

Bees are the messengers of the gods, so protect them. They are a sign of good luck and prosperity.

Hearing an owl hoot is a sign of approaching trouble—but spit three times and the evil will go away.

It is good luck to have a haircut when there is a full moon.

If you see a snake, your family will have some good luck. Even though the snake may be poisonous, do not harm it.

THE PANTHEON

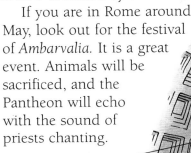

The Pantheon, Rome's temple to all the gods, is one of the most beautiful buildings to be found in Rome, and definitely worth a visit. Rome has a mixture of religions.

As the empire grew, gods from other cultures, such as Greece and Africa, were absorbed into the rich mix of Roman religion. Even the Christians' god is now tolerated by the state.

If you are in Rome around May, look out for the festival of *Ambarvalia*. It is a great event. Animals will be sacrificed, and the Pantheon will echo with the sound of priests chanting.

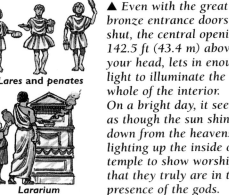

The dome
Weighing more than 5,000 tons, the dome is made from concrete mixed with lightweight pumice stone. The many square recesses helped to reduce the weight, and let the concrete dry out more quickly.

Religion at home
Romans believe their home is protected by spirits. *Lares* are ancestor spirits. They are worshiped at the family's shrine, called the *lararium*, in the living-room. Wine and incense are left there every day. *Penates* are the spirits who protect the family's larder.

Lares and penates

Lararium

▲ *Even with the great bronze entrance doors shut, the central opening, 142.5 ft (43.4 m) above your head, lets in enough light to illuminate the whole of the interior. On a bright day, it seems as though the sun shines down from the heavens, lighting up the inside of the temple to show worshipers that they truly are in the presence of the gods.*

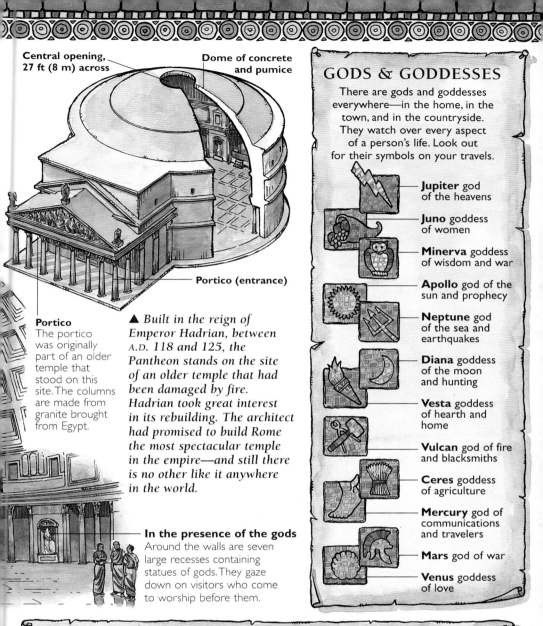

Central opening,
27 ft (8 m) across

Dome of concrete
and pumice

Portico (entrance)

Portico
The portico was originally part of an older temple that stood on this site. The columns are made from granite brought from Egypt.

▲ Built in the reign of Emperor Hadrian, between A.D. 118 and 125, the Pantheon stands on the site of an older temple that had been damaged by fire. Hadrian took great interest in its rebuilding. The architect had promised to build Rome the most spectacular temple in the empire—and still there is no other like it anywhere in the world.

In the presence of the gods
Around the walls are seven large recesses containing statues of gods. They gaze down on visitors who come to worship before them.

GODS & GODDESSES

There are gods and goddesses everywhere—in the home, in the town, and in the countryside. They watch over every aspect of a person's life. Look out for their symbols on your travels.

Jupiter god of the heavens

Juno goddess of women

Minerva goddess of wisdom and war

Apollo god of the sun and prophecy

Neptune god of the sea and earthquakes

Diana goddess of the moon and hunting

Vesta goddess of hearth and home

Vulcan god of fire and blacksmiths

Ceres goddess of agriculture

Mercury god of communications and travelers

Mars god of war

Venus goddess of love

CHRISTIANITY AND CATACOMBS

Before A.D. 313 Christianity was not tolerated in the Roman Empire. Since then, Emperor Constantine has allowed Christians to openly worship their god. As more Romans become Christians, the old gods are becoming less popular.
Along the *Via Appia* you will find underground passages (catacombs) where Christians bury their dead in slots cut into the soft rock.

The fish is a symbol of Christianity. In Greek, the word for fish is *ichthus.* These letters are short for "Jesus Christ, son of God, savior."

Columns

Doric   **Ionic**

Corinthian Tuscan

— capital

— shaft

Composite

— base

Columns can be divided into styles called orders. The Composite and Tuscan orders were invented by the Romans. The others were invented by the Greeks and then copied by the Romans.

Arches

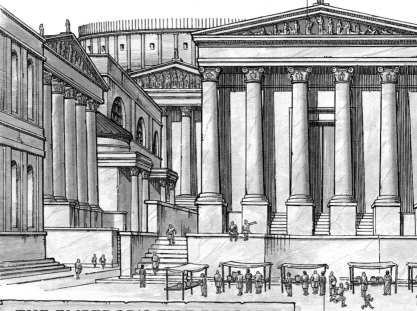

Arch of Constantine
A.D. 312

Triumphal arches celebrate Rome's successes in wars. The Arch of Constantine has two side openings for pedestrians, and a wide central opening for carriages.

THE ROMAN FORUM

The Roman Forum is the city's religious and administrative center. The area is crowded with temples and public buildings, built from the finest white marble. Emperor Augustus (reigned 27 B.C.–A.D. 14) built or restored more than 82 temples here, bringing the marble from the northern quarries at Luna. Later emperors added their own buildings too, as you will see on your visit. It is here that affairs of state are discussed, and where politicians address the public from the *rostra*, a stone platform. If you get the chance, stop and listen—Rome is famous for its great orators.

Temple of Julius Caesar
This temple is one of the oldest buildings in the Roman Forum. It was built by Augustus in 42 B.C. as a memorial to Caesar after his murder in 44 B.C.

THE EMPEROR'S FIRE BRIGADE

After a major fire in A.D. 6, Emperor Augustus created the *vigiles*. It is a fire brigade of 7,000 freed slaves. They use hand pumps to squirt water, and have the power to break into a house if they think it is on fire.

Old market
In earlier times the Roman Forum was the city's market-place, where traders set up stalls to sell their goods.

Pillars and columns

You will see free-standing pillars and columns, celebrating Rome's victories in battle.

WHO'S WHO?

The Roman Forum is a magnet to Romans and non-Romans alike. You will see all sorts of people, especially visitors from Rome's distant provinces, whom you will recognize by their distinctive clothing.

Provincials

Visitors from the provinces wear non-Roman clothes—women from Syria with tall hats, men from Gaul in trousers, and Celtic ladies with woolen shawls.

The poor

Spare some small change for the city's needy poor, enough to buy their daily gruel.

Arch of Augustus

The *Via Sacra*, meaning "the sacred way," is a famous Roman road. It passes right through this arch, which was built by Rome's first emperor, Augustus, in 30 B.C.

Temple of Vesta

◀ *Inside the Temple of Vesta, six Vestal Virgins keep a sacred fire burning day and night. They live in a house next to it, and are the only women priests in Rome. The never-dying fire represents the life of the city of Rome.*

ALL FORUMS TOGETHER

The original Roman Forum (**xi** below) was in a valley between Rome's hills. As the city grew, its shops were gradually moved elsewhere, until only public buildings were left. Successive emperors added new forums, to create this patchwork of temples and basilicas.

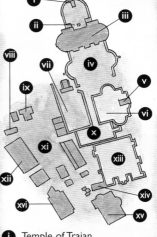

i   Temple of Trajan

ii   Trajan's Column

iii   Basilica Ulpia

iv   Forum of Trajan

v   Temple of Mars Ultor

vi   Forum of Augustus

vii   Forum of Julius Caesar

viii   Temple of Saturn

ix   Temple of Concord

x   Forum of Nerva

xi   Roman Forum

xii   Basilica Julia

xiii   Forum of Vespasian

xiv   Temple of Romulus

xv   Basilica of Constantine

xvi   House of the Vestal Virgins and Temple of Vesta

Fines

For stealing, a person can be sentenced to pay a fine.

Exile

A Roman who chooses to become a citizen of another town, loses his right to remain a citizen of Rome, and is banished from the great city altogether.

Loss of freedom

For avoiding tax or for a military offense, a person can be sold into slavery.

Loss of property

For forging coins or documents, a person's property can be confiscated.

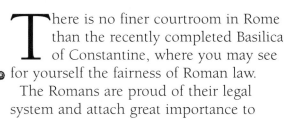

THE BASILICA

There is no finer courtroom in Rome than the recently completed Basilica of Constantine, where you may see for yourself the fairness of Roman law. The Romans are proud of their legal system and attach great importance to it. Cicero, a famous lawyer and public speaker, once said: "The state without law would be like the human body without mind." The law is supreme, and everyone, even the emperor, has to obey it. It is a basic right of a Roman citizen that he or she is presumed innocent until proven guilty in a court of law.

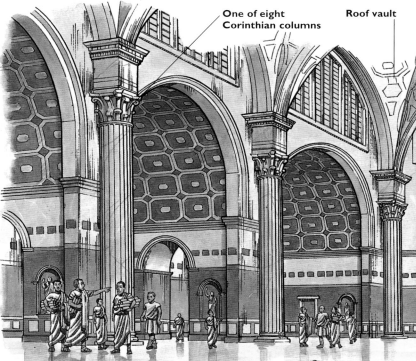

One of eight Corinthian columns

Roof vault

Law in action
After they have listened to the details of the crime, the jury decides whether the accused person is guilty or innocent. Only Roman citizens can be jurors.

▲ *At its highest point, the Basilica of Constantine is 120 ft (36.5 m) from floor to ceiling. Behind the gleaming marble lies a skeleton of brick and concrete, without which the building could not stand. The skill of the architect is in knowing how to place the columns to take the weight and strain of the roof.*

Jurors place wax tablets in an urn

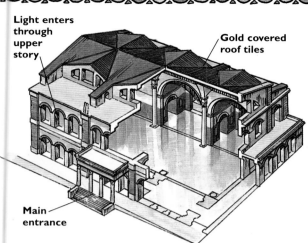

Light enters through upper story

Gold covered roof tiles

Main entrance

Statue of Constantine
In a semicircular recess leading off the main room, known as the *apse*, there is a statue of Emperor Constantine, 39 ft (11.9 m) tall. Its marble eyes seem to follow visitors about.

▲ *The Basilica of Constantine, completed in A.D. 313, can be found beside the Roman Forum. Visitors are amazed at its construction. Three huge marble-faced vaults arch their way across the main room, and the painted ceiling sparkles with gold.*

GUILTY OR NOT GUILTY?

When all the evidence against the accused person has been heard, each juror writes his judgement on a wax tablet and puts it in an urn. He writes one of these:

Accused

A (*absolvo* Not Guilty); **C** (*condemno* Guilty) or **NL** (*non liquet* Not Proven). The verdict is decided by the most number of votes cast.

RULING THE PROVINCES

The empire has never been easy to rule. There has been the constant threat of invasion from barbarians, and uprisings have had to be dealt with in some of the more troublesome provinces.

Governors

Roman law applies to some 50 million people in the empire. Rome's chief official in each province is the governor or proconsul. It is his job to see that the rule of Rome is properly carried out.

Rebellion

When Britannia, Rome's most northerly province, dared to resist Rome, the rebels were swiftly sought out and punished. The same has happened in Judea.

The army

The Roman army is a fearsome fighting machine of well-trained soldiers. Its legions can move quickly into action.

TRAJAN'S MARKETS

All over Rome you will find old inscriptions bearing the name of Emperor Trajan, carved on the many buildings and monuments he gave the city. There can be no doubt that the finest of them all is Trajan's Forum, next to which are Trajan's Markets. Visit the markets to buy fresh food or pick up some souvenirs, or simply take time to wander and soak up the bustling atmosphere of Roman market life.

TRAJAN

Born A.D. 53 in Spain **Died** A.D. 117
Occupation Soldier and emperor (became emperor in A.D. 98)
Married Plotina, a Gaul. No children
Claim to fame Expanded the Roman Empire to its greatest extent; built baths, markets, a forum, and an aqueduct in Rome
Liked Wars, wine, gladiator fights

Main hall
This is where the city's poor come to receive food handouts. Offices for those in charge of the markets are here too.

Statue of Trajan

Brick-faced
The markets were designed to be purely functional, which is why they are built of tough concrete faced with hard-wearing brick.

Spiral staircase with 184 steps

Trajan's tomb

◄ *Trajan's Column of A.D. 113 commemorates his conquest of Dacia. It is almost 100 ft (30 m) high, decorated with military scenes. The scenes are carved on an 800-foot-long (244 m) spiral band, showing more than 2,500 human figures.*

Shops
The shops are cavelike rooms with wide doors. The sign *Salve lucrum* means "Hail, profit!"— a shopkeeper's motto.

▼ *Trajan's Forum is the largest of all the forums in Rome, containing a temple, shops, libraries, and a basilica. It was paid for from the spoils of Emperor Trajan's wars in Dacia, a region north of the Danube River which was part of the empire for a short time.*

Temple of Trajan

Greek library

Trajan's Column

Latin library

Basilica Ulpia

Trajan's Markets

Trajan's Forum

▼ *Trajan's Markets are a multi-story complex of 150 shops and offices, together with a large main hall. They are built on five curving levels, cut into the side of the Quirinal hill.*

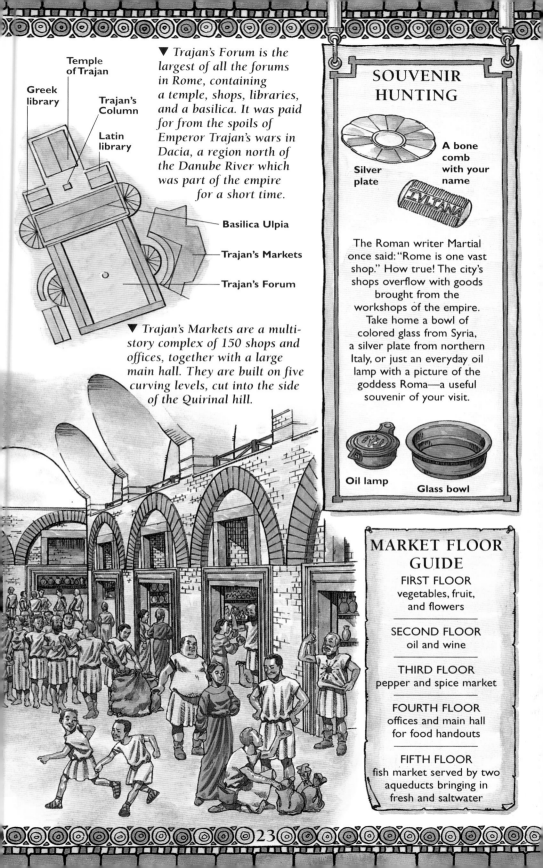

SOUVENIR HUNTING

Silver plate

A bone comb with your name

The Roman writer Martial once said: "Rome is one vast shop." How true! The city's shops overflow with goods brought from the workshops of the empire. Take home a bowl of colored glass from Syria, a silver plate from northern Italy, or just an everyday oil lamp with a picture of the goddess Roma—a useful souvenir of your visit.

Oil lamp

Glass bowl

MARKET FLOOR GUIDE

FIRST FLOOR
vegetables, fruit, and flowers

SECOND FLOOR
oil and wine

THIRD FLOOR
pepper and spice market

FOURTH FLOOR
offices and main hall for food handouts

FIFTH FLOOR
fish market served by two aqueducts bringing in fresh and saltwater

Ovid (43 B.C.–A.D. 18) wrote love poems. Travelers should note that the Christian Church and Emperor Constantine now disapprove of them—but many people still enjoy reading them in secret.

Terence (c. 180–159 B.C.) was a slave from Africa who was educated by his master, and then freed. He wrote six comic plays.

Historians

Tacitus (c. A.D. 55–115) is one of Rome's greatest historians. He wrote about the history of Rome and the first emperors. His books help the Romans learn about their past.

VISIT TO A CITY LIBRARY

Rome has many public libraries, the biggest of which is the Ulpian library, founded by Emperor Trajan, and filled with books written in both Latin and Greek. There are also many small private libraries—indeed, it is a sign of a person's social standing and wealth to have a room filled with books: one citizen boasts a collection of 62,000! You will find books from all the great writers in the city's libraries, but perhaps the greatest works of all are those by Homer, whose stories of old Greece are as exciting today as when he wrote them. Happy reading!

Wooden winding stick or *umbilicus*

Book or *liber*

Grammaticus

▲ *The library, or bibliotheca, contains books written on rolls of paper made from the papyrus plant, which grows along the Nile River in Egypt. The book rolls are stored in wooden bookcases. To help readers find the books they want, each bookcase is numbered, and each roll has a label fixed to it, giving the book's title.*

Reading and rolling
A reader unrolls a little of a book roll at a time. He unrolls with his right hand, and rolls the paper onto the winding stick with his left hand.

▼ A wooden writing tablet is used for everyday messages. It is coated with a thin layer of wax, into which a message is scratched with a metal or bone writing implement called a stylus. Mistakes can be smoothed out with the flat end of the stylus.

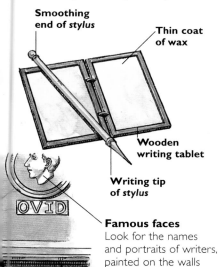

Smoothing end of *stylus*

Thin coat of wax

Wooden writing tablet

Writing tip of *stylus*

Famous faces
Look for the names and portraits of writers, painted on the walls of the library.

Ink mixer
The best black ink, or *atramentum*, is made from three parts of soot, scraped from the walls of furnaces, to one part of tree gum. Add a dash of wormwood to keep the mice away, then bake in the sun until dry. To use, mix with a little water or vinegar.

MAKING A BOOK ROLL

A book roll can be long—there is a 360-foot (110 m) roll in Constantinople, with the works of the Greek poet Homer written on it! Most long books are divided into small rolls, each of about 100 papyrus sheets, joined edge to edge.
The words are written with a pen, dipped into ink. While the ink is still wet, mistakes can be wiped away with a sponge. The last sheet is glued onto a wooden stick, called the *umbilicus*, around which the roll is wound. Clear oil is smeared over the roll to protect it from bookworms.

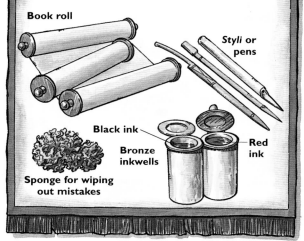

Book roll

Styli or pens

Black ink

Bronze inkwells

Red ink

Sponge for wiping out mistakes

▼ Slaves called librarii *work in a library. They are good at reading and writing. They make books by copying the words from old books onto new book rolls. They try not to make mistakes.*

EDUCATION FOR BOYS AND GIRLS

A boy goes to school between the ages of 7 and 16. He learns reading, writing, math, and public speaking. There are no tables at school, so he rests his writing tablet on his knees, while he listens to the teacher, or *grammaticus*. He might have a *paedagogus*, an educated Greek slave, who acts as his private tutor. A girl goes to school between the ages of 7 and 12, at which age she is able marry. However, many girls do not go to school. Instead, their mothers teach them the duties of house and home.

Paedagogus

Centurion

The commander of a company of 80 men. It is his job to lead them into battle.

Standard bearer

The *signifer* carries a pole, called a standard, from which flies a dragon. It hisses in the wind.

Hornblowers

Soldiers march to the sound of music played by the *cornicines* on woodwind instruments.

Legionnaries

The fighting men of the army are the legionnaries. Each must serve from 20 to 25 years in the army before he is allowed to leave.

VISIT TO AN ARMY CAMP

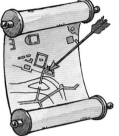

The Roman army is a highly-trained and well-disciplined fighting force. The backbone of the army is its legions, which are units of about 5,000 men. This great army has conquered many lands. Wherever the army has gone, it has built roads and bridges, and has pushed the empire's frontiers ever forward. In Rome, you will see the Praetorian Guard, a group of specially picked soldiers created by Emperor Augustus in 27 B.C. Their job is to protect both the emperor and the city.

Officer in charge
The centurion marches at the head of his troops. The sideways crest across his helmet is a sign of his rank.

Praetorian standard
The standard of the Praetorian Guard differs from most— it has portraits of the emperor inside its disks.

Wooden staff, called a *vitis*, used to punish disobedient soldiers

Metal leg guards called greaves

Hobnailed leather boots called *caliga*

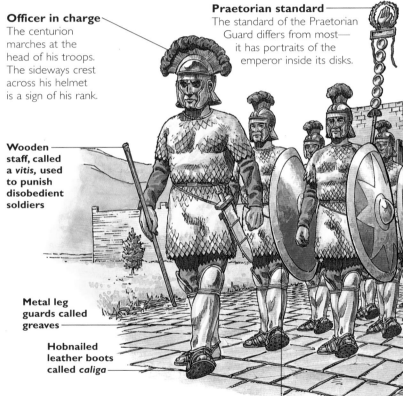

▲ The Praetorian Guard is the chief military force in Rome. Their camp on the north side of the city has room for about 10,000 men. They are paid more than ordinary soldiers, and they only have to serve for 16 years in the army. Because soldiers in the Praetorian Guard lead a comfortable life, soldiers in the rest of the army are jealous of them.

On parade
On your visit look out for the Praetorian Guard as they march out of camp. These soldiers march in neat files, wearing ornate helmets and breastplates, and carrying oval shields.

A SOLDIER'S WEAPONS

Roman legionnaries go into battle with three types of weapon at their disposal—two javelins, a sword, and a dagger. Each javelin is 6 ft 9 in. (205 cm) long, and has an iron point. It bends on impact, so it cannot be reused by the enemy. In hand-to-hand fighting a short sword is used to slash with, and a dagger is used for stabbing.

Javelin or *pilum*

Sword or *gladius*

Dagger or *pugio*

Tower

Camp wall
The concrete and brick wall around the camp of the Praetorian Guard is 10 ft (3 m) high. Every 20 ft (6 m) along the wall is a small, square battlement.

Gate and towers
Soldiers come and go from their camp through heavy wooden gates between two tall towers.

BATTLE TECHNIQUES

Pluteus

When the Romans attack a town, they have many ways of winning a battle. One is to besiege the enemy. The army surrounds the town, trapping the inhabitants inside until they surrender. Soldiers are able to move closer to the town, safe inside a movable *pluteus* or shelter.

Catapulta

In battle, soldiers shoot iron-tipped bolts, like arrows, from catapults. They fly straight and fast, and can travel as far as 1,200 ft (365 m).

Testudo

Soldiers form a *testudo*, meaning "tortoise," by locking shields. They are safe from stones and arrows, and can advance right up to the enemy.

The Roman Empire
When Emperor Trajan died in A.D. 117, the Roman Empire was at its greatest extent. The army had conquered lands across much of western and southern Europe, as well as parts of Africa and Asia. After a conquest, it was the army's job to keep the peace in the new lands.

BRITANNIA
GAUL
HISPANIA
ITALIA
DACIA
ASIA MINOR
AFRICA

The Roman Empire in A.D. 117

RELAX AT THE BATHS

The Roman people believe that a clean body is a healthy body, less likely to fall sick. So, after you've walked the hot and dusty streets of Rome, you'll be ready for a trip to the famous Roman baths. Relax in the cleansing steam and healing waters of the baths, and follow it up with a soothing body massage. And before you leave, why not stay for a bite to eat, or a stroll in the park with a book from the library? There's something for everyone at the baths, especially at Rome's grandest, the Baths of Caracalla, which are large enough to entertain 1,600 visitors at a time. As the Romans say: *Benelava*— "have a good bath!"

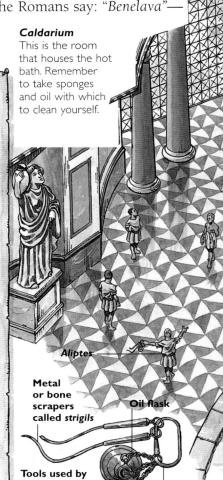

Caldarium
This is the room that houses the hot bath. Remember to take sponges and oil with which to clean yourself.

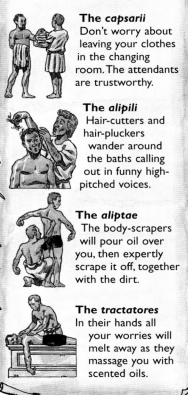

WHO'S WHO?

The *capsarii*
Don't worry about leaving your clothes in the changing room. The attendants are trustworthy.

The *alipili*
Hair-cutters and hair-pluckers wander around the baths calling out in funny high-pitched voices.

The *aliptae*
The body-scrapers will pour oil over you, then expertly scrape it off, together with the dirt.

The *tractatores*
In their hands all your worries will melt away as they massage you with scented oils.

Aliptes

Metal or bone scrapers called *strigils*

Oil flask

Tools used by an *aliptes*

Handle

ENTERTAINMENT

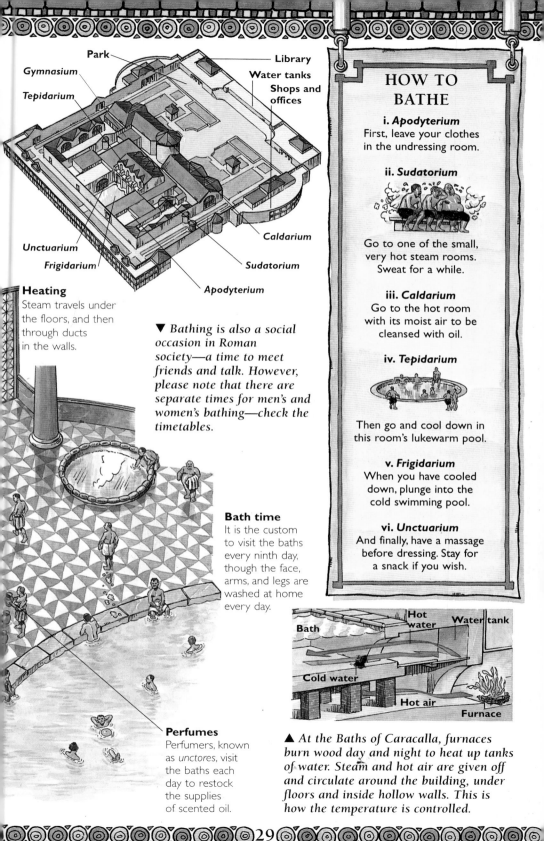

Park
Gymnasium
Tepidarium

Library
Water tanks
Shops and offices

Caldarium
Sudatorium
Apodyterium

Unctuarium
Frigidarium

Heating
Steam travels under the floors, and then through ducts in the walls.

▼ *Bathing is also a social occasion in Roman society—a time to meet friends and talk. However, please note that there are separate times for men's and women's bathing—check the timetables.*

Bath time
It is the custom to visit the baths every ninth day, though the face, arms, and legs are washed at home every day.

Perfumes
Perfumers, known as *unctores*, visit the baths each day to restock the supplies of scented oil.

HOW TO BATHE

i. *Apodyterium*
First, leave your clothes in the undressing room.

ii. *Sudatorium*

Go to one of the small, very hot steam rooms. Sweat for a while.

iii. *Caldarium*
Go to the hot room with its moist air to be cleansed with oil.

iv. *Tepidarium*

Then go and cool down in this room's lukewarm pool.

v. *Frigidarium*
When you have cooled down, plunge into the cold swimming pool.

vi. *Unctuarium*
And finally, have a massage before dressing. Stay for a snack if you wish.

Hot water
Water tank
Bath
Cold water
Hot air
Furnace

▲ *At the Baths of Caracalla, furnaces burn wood day and night to heat up tanks of water. Steam and hot air are given off and circulate around the building, under floors and inside hollow walls. This is how the temperature is controlled.*

LOOK OUT FOR

Actors

All the parts are played by men—except in the *mimus*, or mime. This is a kind of comedy in which women play the female parts and masks are not worn. Actors wear bulky costumes and high shoes to make them appear big.

Musicians

Musicians perform during the play to create an atmosphere for the drama. Listen for flutes, cymbals, rattles, and tambourines.

Scene shifters

They raise and lower pieces of scenery and any backcloths, and operate special effects machines, such as the one that makes the sound of rolling thunder.

THEATER AND MUSIC

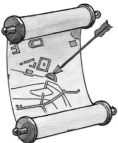

If you're in Rome at the time of a public holiday, you can be sure that the city's theaters will be packed with audiences anxious to see new plays and old favorites. Look out for the *pantomimus* actor, who may come on stage during the performance. Without speaking, he will use dance and movement to tell his part of the play, accompanied by the *chorus*. Performances are held in the afternoons—arrive early to be certain of getting a seat. Once inside, sit close to the stage. That way you'll have no problem seeing or hearing the actors. Sit back and enjoy!

DO'S AND DON'TS

 Don't sit in the emperor's chair of state. You should sit on the stone benches behind it.

 Bring a soft cushion to sit on—the theater's stone seats are very hard.

 In case the theater's sun-shade isn't working, bring a parasol to protect yourself from the sun.

 Bring perfume to sprinkle on your seat, to reduce the bad smell of sweat from those near you.

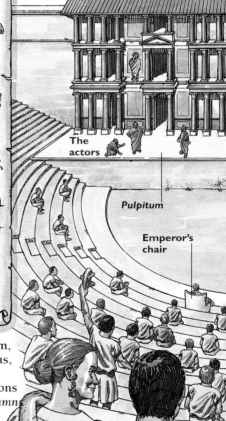

The actors

Pulpitum

Emperor's chair

▶ *Actors appear on the* pulpitum, *or stage, together with the* chorus, *whose members dance and sing. Behind is the painted* scaenae frons *or backdrop, decorated with columns and statues. In front is the semicircular* orchestra, *a space reserved for important spectators.*

THEATER OF MARCELLUS

This is Rome's 12,000-seat open-air theater, built by Emperor Augustus who named it in honor of Marcellus, his son-in-law. It's a great place to see a play, such as the ever-popular *The Menaechmus Brothers*, written by Plautus, one of Rome's funniest playwrights. The play is about identical twins who get mistaken for each other. Comedies by Terence are always good fun—see one if you can.

Tragic (sad)

Comic (happy)

▲ *Actors wear masks in most plays. They show the audience the type of characters they are playing in the performance, such as comic or tragic, young or old, calm or angry. Their large features can be seen by people in the back rows, so it's easy to figure out which character is which.*

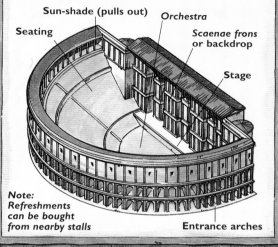

Sun-shade (pulls out)

Orchestra

Seating

Scaenae frons or backdrop

Stage

Note: Refreshments can be bought from nearby stalls

Entrance arches

Scenae frons

The chorus

Pantomimus

Orchestra

Hecklers
At the end of the performance, an actor will say "applaud." Then you'll have to decide whether to clap or hiss—or even throw apples—depending on what you thought of the performance!

APPRECIATION
If you like the play, show your appreciation.

LIKE IT A LITTLE: snap your fingers.

LIKE IT MORE: clap your hands.

LIKE IT A GREAT DEAL: wave the corner of your tunic or a handkerchief.

The wounded

A man dressed as Charon, ferryman of the Underworld, kills the mortally wounded by smashing their skulls with a mallet.

Floggers
If a gladiator is fighting badly, he is flogged until he fights better.

Doctors

They help injured men to recover, so they can live to fight again.

Sand cleaners
They cover up pools of blood with fresh sand.

Facts and figures
• 5,000 beasts were killed on the day the arena opened in A.D. 80.
• 50,000 people can fit inside.
• The sun-shade is like a ship's sail. It needs 1,000 sailors to work it, using ropes and pulleys.
• The Colosseum is also known as the Flavian Amphitheater.

GOING TO THE ARENA

For an exciting day out, visit the Colosseum, Rome's main arena, where you can enjoy some of the empire's favorite sporting events. There is something to suit all tastes, from gladiator fights to animal hunts. Look out for notices painted on walls around the city— they give the details of forthcoming events.

Tickets are distributed before the start of a show—just turn up at the entrance numbered on your ticket, then take the stairs to your seat. At the start of a gladiator show, listen for the brave fighters who say: "We who are about to die salute you!" And when the time comes, it is you who must decide if the defeated gladiator should live or die. If you show no mercy, then join in as the crowd calls out: "*Hoc habet!*"—"Get him!"

DO'S AND DON'TS

Have no mercy! Pointing your thumb down at the end of a fight means "don't spare him!"

Bring money! You'll need it for betting during the games.

Bring your own food! The games last all day, with no stop for a break.

Men and women do not sit together. This is forbidden!

Warning! Don't go if you think the violent shows might make you throw up.

Take your seat
Men sit on the marble-faced front seats. Women and those who cannot afford full-price tickets have to sit on the cheaper wooden seats at the back.

Sun-shade
A gigantic sheet of cloth called the *velarium* can be stretched over the top of the arena to provide shade.

Statues in recesses

80 entrances and exits called *vomitoria*, of which 76 are for public use

GREAT MOMENTS IN THE COLOSSEUM'S HISTORY

Longest running show
In A.D. 116, Emperor Trajan held non-stop games for 117 days, with 10,000 gladiators.

Battles on water
It used to be possible to flood the arena with 5 ft (1.5 m) of water, for ships to fight in battle.

A party to remember
When Rome celebrated its 1,000th birthday, in A.D. 249, all the city's beasts were killed, including 10 tigers.

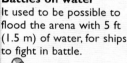

GLADIATORS READY!

Velitis   Retiarius   Secutor

Most gladiators are either prisoners-of-war or criminals. Some are trained in fighting skills at special gladiatorial schools. The better they fight, the more exciting they are to watch.

Velitis ("skirmisher")
Wears no armor. Carries a javelin for throwing at an opponent. Fights with other skirmishers, five against five.

Retiarius ("net fighter")
Wears armor on one arm. Carries a net and a three-pointed fork. Is very fast.

Secutor ("pursuer")
Wears a helmet, leg guards, and armor on his sword arm.

The *podium*
The best seats are right at the front, reserved for the emperor and other important people.

Wooden sword
This is given to gladiators who have fought well. If they are slaves they are made free; if freemen they can retire.

Gladiators fighting on the sand

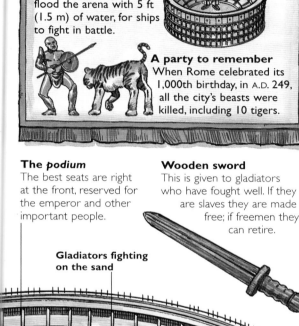

Underground
Beneath the arena is a warren of rooms and cages. Wild animals are kept down here, until it is time to bring them up to ground level. Trapdoors are opened and machines lift the beasts straight into the arena.

Corridors

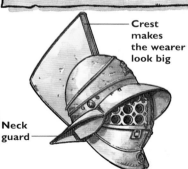

Crest makes the wearer look big

Neck guard

▲ *Gladiators from Samnium, a region to the south of Rome, are the most heavily armored fighters. An image of Hercules, the gladiators' god, is often seen on the front of their helmets.*

A DAY AT THE RACES

Charioteers wear the colors of the companies they work for. There are four companies, or "factions": the Reds, Whites, Blues, and Greens. Diocles was the most famous driver. He came from Spain, raced for the Reds for 24 years and won 1,462 races.

Winner's prizes

A winning driver receives a victor's palm leaf and a purse of gold.

Horses

Racehorses are specially bred in Spain. They are brought to Rome to be trained for the races. Some horses become very famous, such as Victor, who lived up to his name and won 429 races.

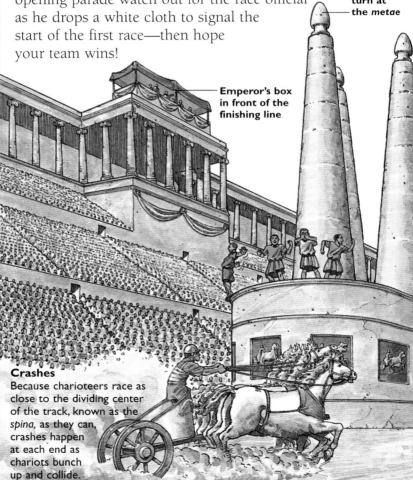

One of the most popular entertainments in the Roman Empire is chariot racing. These events are staged at *circuses*, special buildings with a race track. The *Circus Maximus*, meaning "great circus," is one of the grandest race tracks you will see. Whenever the city holds events at the *Circus Maximus*, you can be sure it will be a sell-out occasion, so try to buy your tickets in advance. If you don't already support one of the chariot teams in the race, choose one before you go. Wear something in the team's colors to show that you support them. After the opening parade watch out for the race official as he drops a white cloth to signal the start of the first race—then hope your team wins!

Chariots turn at the *metae*

Emperor's box in front of the finishing line

Crashes
Because charioteers race as close to the dividing center of the track, known as the *spina,* as they can, crashes happen at each end as chariots bunch up and collide.

▼ Chariots are drawn by either two (biga), three (triga), or four (quadriga) horses. In a race at the Circus Maximus as many as 12 chariots can burst from the starting gates for each race. The chariots have lightweight frames and are richly decorated.

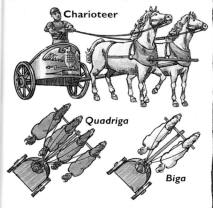

Charioteer

Quadriga

Biga

▼ The chariots race around the track at high speed, in a counterclockwise direction. A race with the powerful four-horse chariots, as shown below, is quite a spectacle!

CIRCUS MAXIMUS

Length 2,000 ft (610 m) **Width** 650 ft (198 m)
Seating 250,000 spectators
Race distance 7 laps of the *spina* (5 miles/8 km)
Race direction Counterclockwise
Number of races per day 24
Refreshments Buy from stalls outside the track
Segregation There is none—men and women are free to sit together

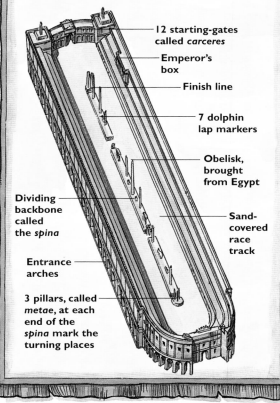

12 starting-gates called *carceres*

Emperor's box

Finish line

7 dolphin lap markers

Obelisk, brought from Egypt

Dividing backbone called the *spina*

Sand-covered race track

Entrance arches

3 pillars, called *metae*, at each end of the *spina* mark the turning places

Winners and losers
People gamble huge sums of money on the result of a race. Victory goes to the winning chariot—whether its driver is still in it or not!

DID YOU KNOW?

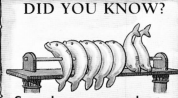

Seven laps, seven markers
One of seven bronze dolphins on the *spina* is turned each time a lap has been completed.

Falx
A charioteer carries a sharp knife called a *falx*. If his chariot crashes, he uses the knife to cut through the reins tied around his body.

ALL ROADS LEAD TO ROME

There are some 53,000 miles (85,300 km) of road in the empire—all leading out from Rome. This road network plays a very important role in Roman life, bringing goods and people to the city from all over the empire. Roads were first used to move soldiers swiftly into new lands, which they claimed for Rome, and were built in straight lines, keeping the distance between places as short as possible. They are now used by many different people—tax collectors, merchants, and travelers like yourself—which explains how the culture of this magnificent civilization has spread so far.

ROAD NETWORK

Via Appia

Capua

Roma
(Rome)

Brundisium
(Brindisi)

Rome is at the center of the road network. In the Roman Forum you will see the Golden Milestone, known as the *Miliarium Aureum*. This was set up by Emperor Augustus. All roads in the country are measured from here.

Milestones
Look out for milestones, which can be up to 6 ft (1.8 m) tall. They are welcome sights to all travelers since you can figure out how much further you have to travel. Their inscriptions tell you the distance to the main towns along the road, as well as each town's distance from Rome.

PORTUS

Port of Claudius

Milestone (15 miles/24 km from Rome)

Port of Trajan

Port of Ostia
Lying at the mouth of the Tiber River, 15 miles (24 km) from Rome, this is the city's original port. An artificial harbor at nearby Portus, built from a special concrete that hardens under water, now handles larger ships than Ostia.

Tombs

Sacred Isle

MARE TYRRHENUM
(Tyrrhenian Sea)

OSTIA

● **Laurentum**

Mile counting machine

If you're traveling a long distance, check to see if your carriage is fitted with an *hodometer*. This clever invention drops a stone into a box each time the carriage has covered one Roman mile. At the end of the journey, count the stones to see how far you've come.

The *Via Appia*

The first road of all was the *Via Appia*. Construction began in 312 B.C. At first, it ran from Rome to Capua, 132 miles (212 km) south, but later it was extended to Brundisium on the southeast coast. The journey from Rome to Capua takes five days.

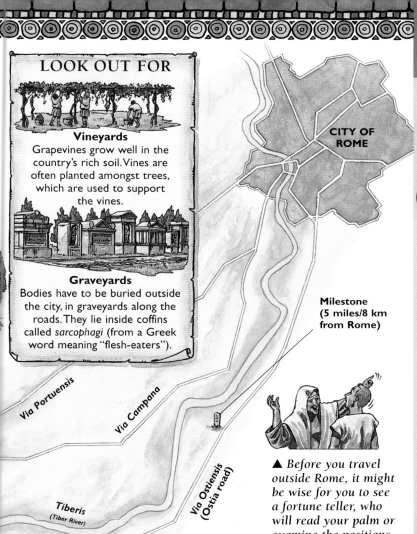

LOOK OUT FOR

Vineyards
Grapevines grow well in the country's rich soil. Vines are often planted amongst trees, which are used to support the vines.

Graveyards
Bodies have to be buried outside the city, in graveyards along the roads. They lie inside coffins called *sarcophagi* (from a Greek word meaning "flesh-eaters").

CITY OF ROME

Via Portuensis

Via Campana

Milestone (5 miles/8 km from Rome)

Tiberis
(Tiber River)

Via Ostiensis (Ostia road)

| 0 | 2.5 km |
| 0 | 1.75 Roman miles (1½ modern miles) |

▲ *Before you travel outside Rome, it might be wise for you to see a fortune teller, who will read your palm or examine the positions of the stars in the night sky. Only then will you know if it is a good time for traveling far.*

3-DAY EXCURSION: ROME TO OSTIA

Day One
Leave at sunrise. Take a carriage along the *Via Ostiensis* to a villa at Laurentum. Arrive lunchtime. Explore nearby beach. Stay overnight at villa.

Day Two
Leave villa early. Head into Ostia. Spend day exploring the shops and squares. Watch boats unloading at the docks. Return to villa for the night.

Day Three
Leave villa before noon for the return trip to Rome. Take water for the journey. Rest in places shaded from the sun. Arrive Rome early evening.

Grapes & olives

Grapes are grown for eating as a fresh fruit, and for turning into wine. Olives are grown for pickling and for their oil.

Wheat

Most of the best farmland is used to grow wheat. The best wheat is *siligo*, which makes a fine white flour for pastries and bread.

Vegetables

Peas, beans, lentils, lettuces, carrots, and radishes grow well here.

Animals

Donkeys pull carts and turn flour-mills; hens, geese, and pigeons give eggs and meat; bees provide honey; sheep, goats, and cows produce milk.

LIFE IN A VILLA

DAY ONE— VILLA AND THE BEACH — Rome — Ostia — The villa

For those Romans who can afford to live in both the town and the country, their country house, or *villa urbana*, is a place to retreat to, away from the noise and dirt of the busy city. The villa built by Pliny the Younger, a famous writer and lawyer, is just 17 miles (27 km) from Rome. It was near enough to the city for him to travel there each day to work. The more common type of country house is the *villa rustica*. This is a home at the center of a large farm. Besides the living rooms for the owner, his farm manager, and all the workers, there are stables, barns, rooms for grinding corn and pressing grapes and olives, cow sheds, and a bakery.

Mosaic floor

Mosaic fitters

▲ There is building work going on in the villa's main courtyard. The owner is having a hard-wearing mosaic pavement laid, with a fashionable geometric pattern. Watch as a worker presses tiny pieces of colored stone called tesserae into soft mortar, carefully following a design drawn on papyrus paper. From time to time he examines the drawing, so he knows which mosaic stones to fit next.

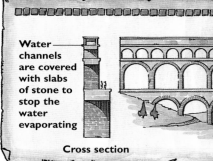

Water channels are covered with slabs of stone to stop the water evaporating

Cross section

Bathroom
Country garden
Turret
Bedroom
Storeroom
Garden
Massage room
Dining room
Beach
Guest room
Main courtyard
Atrium

▲ *The villa urbana of Pliny the Younger is at the coastal town of Laurentum, south of Ostia. You will be staying in the guest room which looks out over the sea. Please close the window shutters if the sea gets rough to keep spray from coming into the room. From the back of the room you will see pleasant woods and mountains in the distance.*

Gardener

AT THE BEACH

The beaches near Ostia, with their fine gray sand, are a short walk from the villa. Because of the area's swamps there are many biting insects there. Eat garlic before you go—as you perspire you will give off a strong garlicky smell and the bugs will stay away!

Dangerous beasts

There are always rumors that wild beasts are loose in the area, having escaped from their cages at Ostia's docks before being sent up river to the arena in Rome. Take care!

Farm workers
Slaves till the fields, tend to the animals, pick the olives, and press the grapes. They are the property of the owner. Life is hard but there are rewards— a slave can be granted freedom by a caring master.

AQUEDUCTS

Water flows inside a channel

Footbridge at lower level

Valley

On your travels you will see Rome's aqueducts, bringing fresh water from rivers and springs. They are skillful works of engineering, rising high above the ground on arches of stone and brick. Water flows gently inside a sloping channel. The slope is so slight you will not notice it. The channel, which is wide enough to crawl inside, is lined with mortar to prevent leaks.

Rope makers

Ropes for ships' rigging, ropes to moor ships to the wharf, ropes to lash cargo to the deck, ropes to tether animals—the list of uses for rope is endless.

Grain weighers

As sacks of grain arrive in the port they are weighed by important officials called *sacomarii*. It is their job to keep detailed records of how much grain there is in the warehouses.

Lighthouse

At night you will see Ostia's flame-topped lighthouse or *pharos*. It is a welcome sight for ships as they approach the port, signaling that their journey is almost over, and guiding them safely to the wharf.

DAY TWO— EXPLORE OSTIA

Rome

Ostia

Ostia, Latin for "mouth," is so called because of its position at the mouth of the Tiber River. It is the commercial port of Rome, and ships from every part of the Roman Empire bring valuable cargoes here. There is no more precious cargo than grain. Some 400,000 tons are shipped to Ostia every year, all to feed the people of Rome. Much grain comes from North Africa, which is a 15- to 20-day voyage across the *Mare Internum*. A late or missing ship is enough to trigger famine and riots in the capital. The people of Ostia live in cramped conditions, and outbreaks of fever are common because of the nearby swamps—take care while you are there.

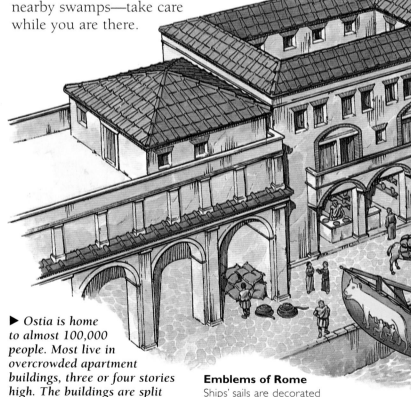

▶ *Ostia is home to almost 100,000 people. Most live in overcrowded apartment buildings, three or four stories high. The buildings are split into groups of small rooms. They don't have water and are dismal places to live.*

Emblems of Rome

Ships' sails are decorated with Rome's emblems, the she-wolf and the twins Romulus and Remus.

HEADING TO ROME

Slaves are the most valuable commodity of all. They arrive at Ostia and are sold in the town's slave markets. Some go to cruel masters who only think of them as speaking tools. They work as laborers on farms. Others may go to kind masters who take care of them, and occasionally they are given back their freedom. Educated Greek slaves work as household secretaries, and are put in charge of educating the sons of the family.

TRADING IN THE PORT

Beasts of the wild

Animals trapped in the wild are brought to Ostia from all over the empire. All are sent to Rome, where fights are staged in the city's arenas. Beasts from Africa are especially sought after, although they are becoming harder to find. There is always demand for lions, boars, and elephants.

Luxury goods

Merchant ships from Alexandria, the port of Egypt, bring much needed grain to feed the people of Rome. Luxury goods from China, India, and Africa, such as silk, spice, incense, and ivory, are also shipped to Ostia from Alexandria.

Apartment building and shops

Merchant ships
Sea-going sailing ships have wide bodies for carrying large cargoes below and on top of the deck. Ships are powered by the wind.

Warehouses

River boats
Small boats are loaded up with grain. It is these boats that transport the grain the 15 miles (24 km) up the Tiber River to the warehouses in Rome.

◀ The most common drink in Rome is wine. As you walk along the harbor at Ostia, look out for large storage pots which are used to transport the city's favorite drink. The best wines are from Greece.

LANGUAGE

The language of the Romans is Latin. Wherever the Roman army has gone, the Latin language has gone too. Today, Latin is spoken all over the Roman Empire, so no matter where you are traveling to or from, if you speak and read Latin you will be understood. It's called Latin because it developed in the part of Italy called Latium, the home of the people called Latins. The Latin alphabet has 23 letters. Most of the letters are based on those used by the Greeks, who began to use the alphabet about 200 years before the Romans did. The letters of the Latin alphabet are:

USEFUL PHRASES

For visitors who cannot speak Latin, the following words and phrases will come in handy. If you say all the letters in the Latin words, you will not go far wrong with the pronunciation, and should be understood.

Hello	*Salve!*
Goodbye	*Vale!*
Thank you	*Bene facis*
Yes/No	*Ita/Non*
How much?	*Quot?*
Where?	*Ubi?*
When?	*Quando?*
Less/More	*Minus/Plus*
Good/Bad	*Bonus/Malus*
How much further?	*Usque quo?*
Where are the lions?	*Ubi sunt leones?*
Have you got food?	*Cibum habes?*

You will see Latin inscriptions all over the place—even on floors of houses. The above mosaic reads *cave canem*, which means "beware of the dog!"

SENDING A LETTER

The Romans have the best postal system in the world, called the *cursus publicus*, which makes use of the 53,000 miles (85,300 km) of roads that crisscross the empire in all directions. Letters travel by courier from stopping-place to stopping-place along the roads. If you do want to send a letter home you'll have to make good friends with a courier. He should only carry business letters from members of the government or the army—but for a small payment you might be able to persuade him to take a letter for you. On a good day a letter can travel about 50 miles (80 km). Visitors from Britannia (Britain), Rome's most northerly province, can expect their letters to take about 30 days to reach home, because they have to cross the *Mare Britannicum* (the English Channel).

THE ROMAN CALENDAR

The Romans use a calendar instituted by Julius Caesar in 46 B.C. It is one of the Romans' greatest achievements because now the months match the seasons of the year. Each year has 365¼ days divided into 12 months. The odd quarter day is accounted for once every four years by adding an extra day to the month of February, so that in that year there are 366 days. This calendar replaced the old one in which the year only had 355 days—ten days too few—which meant that farmers did not know when to plant their crops because the calendar was up to six weeks out of place with the seasons! In honor of Caesar's great work, the seventh month of the new year was named *Julius* after him.

THE ROMAN YEAR

Month	Named after...
Januarius	Janus, god of the doorway. Looks forward to the new and backwards to the old.
Februarius	*Februare* meaning "to cleanse."
Martius	Mars, god of war.
Aprilis	*Aperire* meaning "to open." The month when flowers open.
Maius	Maia, goddess of summer.
Junius	Juno, queen of the gods.
Julius	Julius Caesar, the month of his birth.
Augustus	Augustus, Rome's first emperor.
September	*Septem*, the seventh month in the old Roman calendar.
October	*Octo*, the eighth month in the old Roman calendar.
November	*Novem*, the ninth month in the old Roman calendar.
December	*Decem*, the tenth month in the old Roman calendar.

FESTIVALS

Roman festivals are ancient and go back to the early days of Rome when most people were farmers—this is why the festivals are so concerned with land and animals. Festivals are also public holidays. Listed here are just a few of them—the Romans have about 200 public holidays a year!

January—*Compitalia*
A three-day festival marking the end of the farming year.

March—*Fordicidia*
Cattle are sacrificed to make sure the soil will produce good crops.

21 April—*Parilia*
Rome celebrates her birthday.

May—*Ambarvalia*
A purification festival before the first harvest.

October—*Fontinalia*
A water festival. Springs and wells are decorated with flowers.

17 December—*Saturnalia*
In honor of the god Saturn. Masters change places with their slaves, and parents give toys to their children.

PUBLIC NOTICE!

Visitors should note that the Romans have only recently started using seven days to the week. They have been doing this since A.D. 313, when Emperor Constantine passed the Edict of Milan, allowing Christians to practice their religion. The seven-day week is of Jewish origin. Before this time, the week had eight days, and as old habits die hard, you might find some citizens still working the old way.

COINS & MONEY

For many years the Romans have had a problem with runaway price inflation. Prices for everyday essential goods have kept going up and up. For example, in A.D. 300 a loaf of bread cost 1,000 times more than it had just 25 years earlier! Something had to be done otherwise people would go back to bartering—swapping goods for other goods. This had not been done in Rome for about 600 years. Emperor Diocletian (reigned A.D. 284–305) attempted to put the situation right. He introduced new gold, silver, and copper coins. But people saved the gold and silver and only spent the copper coins. Prices still kept rising. Diocletian then fixed maximum prices for goods such as wheat, wine, and meat. However, all that happened was that people stopped taking goods to market. With fewer goods on the market things got even more expensive. Thankfully, the situation in the Roman Empire is much better now. Under Emperor Constantine (reigned A.D. 307–37) prices have settled down and coins are being used again—except silver ones, which are now out of fashion.

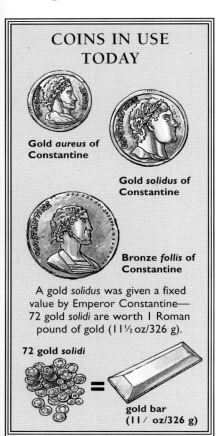

COINS IN USE TODAY

Gold *aureus* of Constantine

Gold *solidus* of Constantine

Bronze *follis* of Constantine

A gold *solidus* was given a fixed value by Emperor Constantine— 72 gold *solidi* are worth 1 Roman pound of gold (11½ oz/326 g).

72 gold *solidi* = gold bar (11/ oz/326 g)

WEIGHTS & MEASURES

Libra	A Roman pound weight (11½ oz/326 g)
Sextarius	A measurement for liquid and corn (0.12 of a gallon/0.45 l)
Iugerum	A measurement for an area of land (120 ft by 240 ft/36 m by 73 m)
Pes	A Roman foot (11.6 inches/29 cm)
Mille passus	A Roman mile (1,618 yards/1,480 m) made up of a thousand *passus* (double paces of five Roman feet)
Stadium	One eighth of a Roman mile (202 yards/185 m)

CHECK YOUR CHANGE!

Beware of cheats! Check against these pictures to see if you've been given a worthless old coin like these.

Emperor Augustus
(27 B.C.–A.D. 14)

Emperor Nero
(A.D. 54–68)

ROMAN NUMERALS

The Romans use seven signs to write all their numerals:

I	V	X	L	C	D	M
1	5	10	50	100	500	1,000

Number	Numeral	Name
1	I	unus
2	II	duo
3	III	tres
4	IV	quattuor
5	V	quinque
6	VI	sex
7	VII	septem
8	VIII	octo
9	IX	novem
10	X	decem
20	XX	viginti
30	XXX	triginta
40	XL	quadraginta
50	L	quinquaginta
100	C	centum
200	CC	ducenti
300	CCC	trecenti
400	CD	quadringenti
500	D	quingenti
1,000	M	mille

Numerals above 1,000 are written with bars above them. The bar shows the numeral is to be multiplied by 1,000. So:

$\overline{V}$ 5,000 $\overline{X}$ 10,000

If the bar has tails, the numeral is to be multiplied by 100,000. So:

$\overline{V}$ 500,000 $\overline{X}$ 1,000,000

Numerals are written in a line, side by side, starting with the highest numeral and working down to the smallest. They are added together. So:

III $1+1+1 = 3$ VII $5+1+1 = 7$

LXXVII $50+10+10+5+1+1 = 77$

If a smaller numeral comes before a larger numeral, the smaller numeral is subtracted (taken away) from the larger one. So:

IV $5-1 = 4$ IX $10-1 = 9$

MCMXCIV $1,000+(1,000-100)+(100-10)+(5-1) = 1,994$

Emperor Domitian
(A.D. 81–96)

Emperor Trajan
(A.D. 98–117)

Emperor Hadrian
(A.D. 117–38)

Emperor Valerian
(A.D. 253–60)

Emperor Aurelian
(A.D. 270–75)

ANCIENT ROME INDEX